As Good As Mango

As Good As Mango

Anand Prahlad

Stephen F. Austin State University Press
P.O. Box 13007, SFA Station
Nacogdoches, TX   75962-3007
sfapress@sfasu.edu

Manufactured in the United States of America

LIBRARY OF CONGRESS IN PUBLICATION DATA
Prahlad, Anand
As Good as Mango / Anand Prahlad

p. cm.
ISBN: 978-1-936205-35-6

1. Poetry. 2. African American Studies 3. Prahlad, Anand.

The paper used in this book meets the requirements of ANSI/NISO Z39.48-1992 (R1997) (Permanence of Paper)

ACKNOWLEDGMENTS

A sincere thanks to the editors of the following journals, who first acknowledged some of the poems in this book.

"Wild" and "Ma Nan" appeared in *Black Magnolias;* "The Harvest" appeared in *Natural Bridge;* and "Neon, Los Angeles" appeared in *Spectrum.*

CONTENTS

Part I

Part 2

As Good as Mango
Part 1

(In Movements and Incantations)

For Kahlil, and Karen Michele, with love always.

As Good as Mango

apple is
the mother of earth.

as good as mango,
as good
        as cassava.

they think it's their seeds
        in her belly,
but they're mine.

look how black
        they are.

look at nappy
        eve and adam.

so apple is
the mother of earth.

out of apple loins
sprang
        ore and fire.

sprang drum and
        tango,

and sun as ripe
        as hulls of
slave cargo.

***

passage

toward the center
of space
      drifts

the vortex
      of pollen.

dead zygote
filling endless

silence, as what
      was once nectar

crystallizes
      in traumatized flesh.

what was once
      equatorial

moves into
      the first winters.

pockets of
empty wind

echo through acacia,
      cassia and cola.

goat's skin
      and guava

scents bubble
      like ppd

under black skin,
  lysogenic,

humming.
  splitting again

each time
the ship rocks

and Africans dis
  embody, spirits

floating above
  the boat, lost

like raptured
  shadows.

     * * *

asha

in the shade of palms
resting

on the long
march to sea

she gnaws her wrist
off.

she flees but
they catch her,

a trail of blood
dust like coal
ash cutting snow.
a white man

patches her up.
not quite knowing

what to call her,
what to call them.

he gave her water
and an apple.

the lions
       don't eat apple,

but the earth
       will eat lions.

       the earth will
welcome mother back.

       bloody hands
of houngans

and sangomas
       danced across

       Africa, casting
spells in trance.

out of the spells
sprang

        spores
and out of
        the spores
        zombies.

white men were
        the zombies

who left
        their souls

in africa
in
        bird bellies
and
        stones
and
        stems
in lizards
        and seeds.

        white means
to have
        a portable heart.

you can take it but
        too seldom do

for some
        unknown reason.

                        ***

smithy

this day dawns
in New Orleans.
in Charleston.
the blacksmith
hides secrets
in the bell.
in the fences
and stairways
and iron gates
laced delicately
as the flights
of cranes.
they whisper
when cows walk.
they summon.
they call out to the fields.

the smithy fire
crackles
and through the crack
in the door
blue rays violet
gold and silver
glimmer.
waves whirl
      and stir
moments
      of ascent.
build then
cascade down
like rapids,
like current down
a ground cord

leaving odors
of hyacinth
and drips
of dance, and gone
just like that, with
someone humming
swing low
someone ringing
the big bell,
the stars out and
venus, he
shudders, sits
down and eats
his bread.

***

ma nan

From side
the white
adobe house
where a wooden
bench sat
in shade.
to the white sand
of the rose garden
with its
staked trellises,
she eases
her large body
between rows
while the preacher
        preaches

about sinners
missing from
      the sanctuary,
exploding
in sweat like
a pummeled boxer.
      She picks
the heady
perfume of plants,
imbibes
their shadows
      like loas
and whispers
Come
Papa Damballa,
just over
my shoulders.
bless the gate,
the portals
and thank you
for
the infinite gift
that led us
safely
out of the garden.
She picks and
drops
the petals in
apron folds
swaying
and later
you can
hear her to
candle flame
chanting

through ripples
of incense before
the altar,
        ring
of hyacinth
for obedience.
clove
of nutmeg
for peace.
        bone
of a white dove.
a whale's tooth.
bough
        of cedar
essence
of rosemary.
vial of vanilla
rose water.
        play on
                drummers.
        zodiac oil
and eagle
feathers
        frankincense
and myrrh
        carnelian
lapis fire
        burning
agate
into gem,
        play fire
                drummers.
play on.
                ***

the spirits

just suppose
the spirits
live here
in seashells (their
ships)   and sleep
by the sea.
the gulf.
the shores of Alabama.
just suppose
they make a sound
like castanets.
that one by one
they come to look
for those with
purple auras.
in the cotton
in the sumac
in the hay in the
stable   in the song
that bends
like a willow
in the body that smells
of mugwort and sweet
milk   tobacco
and sassafras
and corn.
just suppose
they come
for those whose
pain can never
name them.
for those who
would leave

this blood feast,
this subterranean
memory
bitter sweet as
seagrapes,
this other side
of things
now so familiar,
            even
the bludgeoned
beauty of it.
            the blue green
water with its
infectious
            flat horizon
sloshing against
sand and rocks.
the cranes
lifting
            out of marshes.
the audacity
            of white gulls
soaring while they
drown in
            burnt
indigo
            and chains.
this body. the others
like it.
these hopes.
these reasons
to go on.
just suppose
they come for those
with loas dancing

in their pores,
        dancing
on the edge of cliffs,
making out
with new partners.

                                        ***

j o n a h

apple is
the mother of earth.

of this.
and that.

and this is pieces
        this is
                bits
this is   always
just missing
the ibis
trailing
        in his shadow.
this is   blue
        and black
and catch a train
shango
        a shango
yemanja
this is   close
the shutters, like
in a western
        when
        the bad guys

come.
this is   relentless
pain of so far
out the heart
          stops.
          jonah
don't be blue.
don't be pale
          in comparison.
here in the belly
of ogun
remember
gourd
kumina, cuba
oh jonah
don't be blue
even if the Southern is
just another
ship,
even if the Flying Crow
the Santa Fe
or the Dog is
just another
dirty bowels while
crossing crossroads
come
flag a my train
shango
          a shango
yemanja
          jonah
don't be blue
     even as
the wheatfields
go by and you can

never own them
the corn rows
go by
and the orange groves
go by
and the lemon trees
go by
and the orchards
go by
lit like candles --
they don't
own them either.

***

ginger

Ginger
and curry

heal you
             mr and
             mrs jones

red pomegranate
white milk
of coconut

sizzling and
exploding like starburst
like trees
like bark
like stones
like fungus roots

all cumming
hard in your belly.
and apple is
the mother of earth.

saffron sweet rice
yams and jicama

heal you
            shaqueetha
            and teneka

wild greens and lemon
like mango rind
like pure water
like a song sending
ultraviolet
rainbows
through chakras
            re uniting
                        meridians
with the
white hot center

heal you
            abdul and ali.

you can't
find no more
ashanti drum
heart.
terra cotta
guitar strings
snap and

crumble like
bridge
suspensions
half way cross.
you can't
find no more
salves in
peg leg boxes
pins and
wires and
hammers
walking of their
own accord.

piano keys
            to what?

some heavenly
release?

cilantro
and chili peppers

heal you
            sister carrie and
            decon and
            dr smith

from
            slave breath
            and echoes
            in the gametes,
            the marrow.

somedays

when the black
        body
            spreads out
among lotuses
                and lilies,
when the woman
in the moon
            descends
wearing sapphire
and animal tusks
with rivers and stars
gushing from
her navel,

and ginger and pepper
is burning you
and greens is rocking
you on the atlantic
you can swallow
rose and petunia
swallow
            the flesh
of tulip bulb
like peaches
with salt, or a jar
of lilacs, opened
while a pine
wind blows
through windows.

                    ***

aunt lucy

and what about
cherokee
about seminole
about mataponi?
did we feed,
starve, did we?
did we eat apple?
slave lucy came
and stayed a slave
in wigwam and
moccasins.
better yes. better
yet. but still.
about that.
someone gave her
new name a
name. Wabina
Crane Feather.
someone gave her
babies.

Wabina fed on
fish tails. on seeds.
she limped.
she was not so
                strong.
bee songs around
apple trees
healed broken bones.
whips scars.
she hardly ever
spoke. less
and less

touched her.
even the babies.
she tried to sing
to them like bees.
soon enough
they left her alone
humming.
some spirit came
through feather tips,
blue flame, sage
smoke and juniper.
some unfamiliar
spirit.
      she wanted
orunmilla,
      drum talk, even
brer rabbit,
blue fife or juba.
not chamomile,
      though, or rose
hips, sassafras,
not just low moans
of loons and herons –
at least
she still had a mojo.
      but
the way he spoke
her names, all them,
the way he saw into
her, like water,
the way he took her
she went.

         ***

the lynching

at first
he just shook.
and then
he stayed still.
at first
there was
so much pain that
no one there
and no one
       since
would ever be
without it.
but then
he felt
the garden.
          he rolled
torch after torch
and lifted
them to
the ancient urns
lining the cavern.
he lit them
and watched
them break
      the dark
like bullets tear open
flesh, and he ran,
        not outward
or away, but further
down into
      the stamen
           and pistil
where strands

of light
blew back and forth
    and filaments
coiled like conch
spirals
    covered
    with pollen,
sifting down
like coastal mist.
where aqueducts
    lay open
like mouths filled
with insatiable
hunger
for the real
thing
the memory is of.

past mother.
past mama.
past nana.
clear as water.
    past eyeball
moons in
scorched skies.
the sounds of
    liquids
dripping
from the walls.
a fog
    through a valley
of seeds
pulsing like
fat, blue hearts,
and the hummingbird

ripping them open
with its long
slender beak.

        there was
        nowhere else
he could go.
there was no heaven.
there was nothing
he could do
        in fact
there was
        nothing solid
even
as a dream,
all
        just missing
notes, suspended
tingling
like the lip
        of a marigold.

there was
not even
a wall to echo
a scream.
or mind
to think the wail
into being.
        there was just
the body the fire
couldn't touch
and the flowers
        turning emerald
and bright

yellow patches
          prismed,
water rushing
splotches bursting
from a source
touched
          previously
only in
scattered moments.

a long night
of hot embers,
the roaring of the crowd.

and then
the rising
of pre-dawn
          continents
as cocoons
and gardens
          crickets
clouds cowslips
          and clover hummed.

Part 2
Hoodoo

Parrot

livid, she
stooped whenever
he spoke.

let it curl back
into herself
splitting her heart.

we cringed when
her meek smile
mustered.

the claps rung
when it was time
and the song
always came.

the deafness followed.
she felt
dumb as an ostrich.

and let it curl back
into herself.
the parrots
of the jungle

became her cries.
so piercing that
when she stood
before god

even he must have
broke down
and wept.

Ohio

Along
the Ohio turnpike
at dusk

hawks sit in bare
lone trees.
Hereford calves

draw close to
white board fences.
The sun's

last rays
glint off the sides
of Strohs beer trucks

moving by
doing eighty.
Hawks till the air

above green fields.
"Bring the butter"
she yells out.

The Harvest

The harvesting of cows
begins in the morning.

A man standing in the dusk
smokes a cigarette.

Tomorrow's deaths come
to him, like a neighbor's

evening grill smoke
sweetly on the wind.

There is milk and blood
all over the barns,
all over the fences.

There are bits of bone
all over the corn.

There are voices
in the twilight you can
hardly hear, saying
nothing ever happens.

Magna Carta

our magna carta signed,
the larkspur and
gladiolas thick.
the cell phone ringing.

mosquitoes and crepe
myrtle, the sap of
pines oozing upward.
night and the darkness

like milk pouring down
our throats, bits
of tarnished iron.
we gag, choke.

white bird bones,
black bird blood
bearing new mojos.
at least they will soar.

you send the bees home,
and go away too,
leave honey dripping.
leave sewing kits,

leave the coo and
wings of pigeons.
leave skins and brown
stones in the sun.

Manifesto

the long sought after manifesto
arrived in the colonies today.
they thought it would cure all ills
but it didn't. it told them there would be
no more women until the settlement
was built, and it warned against
the sins of relations with the Indians.
no one wanted to say they were
disappointed. so they polished
their guns and drank themselves
to sleep. but still they had no peace.
they could hear the sounds of wolves, owls.
the twigs crackling under cougars.
they could feel the breaths of Cherokee.
when deer came to them in dreams, they shot them.
they all dreamt together they were faceless,
grouped and posing for a photo, lost stories,
bared skulls violently weeping.

Smudged

oh and the night
is so on our faces!
like web, clinging
smudged, saltwind

and chemicals, soot.
even in the daytime,
rouge of prostitutes,
bus sweat, factory

fumes, are a net
thrown over us.
our decadent tongues,
always fishing.

we are in love
with the bitterness
of it, an artificial
wild flavor, or mad

from the beginning,
creating an hour
such as this
so we could say

we are mad because
living in the hour
before our deaths
has made us so.

even the remains
leak their scent
when dollars
become worthless

and our lives
turn cyber.
neons light us up,
we burn like torches.

Dragonfly

dragonfly ocean
sand and salt
the gulls screaming
over white sails.

southern flesh seed
afraid of sea
anemone waters kelp
jellies and lobsters.

cracked crab shells
mussels and wood
drift her big thighs
trim the ocean, stem

her up from it
like mamas tulips.
the thin heads of
children tip waves.

kite comes cruising
coolly over tracing
currents in air
and she is walking

halting wading in it
strum fragile wings
hum, the piercing
wet splayed scream.

Priming

Meditation leaves the mind
will-less as a leaf.

So read
to prime the pump.

Swallow the ink
and spit it back out.

Mind talks to mind-
to what else?

Spokes
sing to other spokes.

Give unto Caesar
what is his,

even this,
the finest of arts.

The Fetishist Weds

In bed, I just think
of worms. Of bones.
The air disappears
when the lights go out. Cold,
wet leaves fall on me, and I wither
like a baby.

I fall asleep and dream
of our white skulls on the sink
next to the glasses
and the wedding cake.

Laying on the beach
always made me hard.
The unbridled roar of wind and
forced feeding of salt.
Even warming my hands around
a homeless fire, I felt, well,
like a man.

Or lying in the park,
speaking in tongues, while
snakes slithered from me.

Sometimes a girl's feet
would come by,
naked as a priest
or nuns without robes.

I would soar like crows over a
foggy morning field. Or gulls
far, far out to sea.

I would fall down, drunk,
and then ascend, triumphant
as Jesus.

Dresses

fly and flow and billow
cling and carpet and sheets.
kites and wings and
ribbons and curtains
and sashes and drapes.
rustles and whistles
and silk and pleated
wails and whispers and whimpers.
cocoons and linen shouts.
rain hiss and waves
and grave hurricane
mouths and red flames
crackling on a pyre.
screeching of rails.
popping of live wires
and a seized chair rocking.
spirits that forget, then
rise. wind blossoms in oaks.
borders that border on
openness, but stay shut,
stay still, stay closed.
borders that surrender
to sound, to hind sights
to cursing holy ghosts.
wrappers and unwrappers.
breezes and breaths
away and against.
flags, and sails, look!
they are screaming.
they are sailing away,
they are singing,
they are melting blue
space and peeling like
ancient photographs.

Missing

When someone is gone
and the house is still
does the wandering
jew have no relationship
with the missing
claret of our blood
or the warmth, or objects
like the jar on the
kitchen table hard against
hard? Our lives go out
like spores on the wind
out of season, apart
from the things we touch
and we miss so dearly
and feel somehow
they must miss us.
The t-shirt on the
carpet soft against
another soft. The plastic
things. The cold phone
on the kitchen formica.
Are the steel screws
holding cabinet knobs
warmed by the wood?
The sink by the
memory of my blood?
The bed sheets by
the memory of my body?
Does the tea cup remember
my lips, or what is was like
on the long boat ride
from China?

Neon, Los Angeles

thru palm trees
the blue neon from
a block away
twenty stories up
washes over us.
the houses and cars
the mini lawns
the sedate plantations.
the hum of it
is imagined
in our sleep
along with the effervescent
urge to get up
and go home all night.

Steam Liners

steamliners, oneliners and
headliners. the altar.
thai and szechwan
atop the transam building
transpacific. transatlantic.

array of christmas
lights along the mother
bridge leading into the city
wink at skyscrapers
in the distance, lit like
transvestites winking back.

rats in the sewer. rats along
the metro rails. gateways
near the golden gate separate
jungle musics from, from
the hills? separate cop heaving
muther, scrunching skulls,
crunching scrotums left
and right, from capital.

tourists from majorca.
new yorkers returning home.
macy's crystal on decks
wash out to sharks in
the flood. your power
goes out. genuine puruvian
art slides down canyon
slopes.

Passing to Point Reyes

Processions pass through here and
down soft winding slopes
of sand and iceplant.

Past rows
of quaint art shops,
preserved with peeling paint.

Past antiques and crafts,
purslane, and
the obligatory, rusted pick-up.

Past a studio
with skylights, and dancers
stretching into petals,

like amputees, reaching,
or trees bending away
from the coast.

Past a sea-green light,
a piano.
A scent like southern magnolia.

Past an aging, black woman,
perfumed and
wearing a sequined sweatband.

Her hands shake.
She smells stale.
She reminds you of someone.

As you draw closer,
there's a precipice
of brightness you slowly fall off.

Ghosts

I remembered the stairs.
They were steep, white.
The third one was broken.
There was sunlight slanting
between fence boards
separating old Victorians.
There were roses and callas.

I remembered scarlet
breaths like wind
through Japanese maples.
The giant windows
that never closed flush.
Hardwood squeaking and
an old, steam heater
clicking like a clock.

I remembered the screech
of iron street car
wheels, when voices
no longer came through
cracks. Then the silence,
like the moment under an
overpass, driving in rain.

I remembered my father.
I would see him whenever
I went home, although,
he would hardly speak.
I hadn't started seeing
his ghost yet blossoming
around my face.

I remembered walking
to the yellow corner store
for bread and milk and
wanting never to forget.
I could remember me
remembering things
without writing a poem.

The Egg Thief

Musacked Penny Lane
floats through air laden
with raw beef and fish scents.

As soon as no one looks
he opens a crate of eggs.
A look comes over his face.

He seems to laugh, on stage
like this, an easy sleight of
hand in front of mamas.

In front of store cams
and cell cameras and secret
button cams and kids,

he slides another one deftly
into his coat. He mocks
our recipe for living.

So pleased with himself,
he almost bows, but to whom?
Not knowing ruins it.

Watching the Internet Reality Show

Forget the background glimpse
of white linens. Wicker
baskets. Stained carpet full of cat's hair.

Forget the walking tattooed pages
of print. The nose rings, nipple needles,
bone pierced brows or lobes,

foreskins or chained linked labias
bright as begonias.
Forget the red velvet thongs

swaying on the bathroom mirror.
A fat belly like a wet fish agape
flopping over a sparkling sink.

Forget the grating, fuzzy pitch of
guitar notes that echo with apocalyptic
ire. Just turn the volume down.

But note the other things so strangely
out of whack. The thing you just
can't touch with your finger.

Note the ghosts you feel but
don't believe in. But first
you have to shut it down.

And then you have to wait while
it crackles and pops itself off.
Now listen, and you can feel them

churning in your belly. Now
you can feel yourself floating like
a shadow, and the world you once

knew as it slowly falls apart.
We used to live by maxims that told us
who we were. We used to say

A picture doesn't lie. But it does now.
The picture steals the soul.
But now, it creates, it incubates it.

Email Makes us all New Yorkians

email makes us all new yorkians,
but some are better at it.

the easy blend of haute and street.
of fire and ice.

everything coming back fast,
like a finger pop in your face.

but mostly, you are in so deep
you couldn't get out,

even if you wanted to.
which is ok, because you don't.

surrounded. being touched.
breathing in others' breaths.

forever home, but never quite.
and never quite asleep.

hours are the new days.
minutes the new winter months.

in new york, you can smell the city.
even if you are blind,

you can still hear it.
you can close your eyes

and listen or daydream,
or hold your breath under water.

when people spit out words,
grammar is always correct,

syntax and diction are always
as sweet as train notes.

when people speak in new york,
they step into suits

as bright as those of mardi gras,
so much older, though.

when people speak in new york
others know what they mean.

So

You like "so's" to make points.
I like them for their transient beauty,
wafered between statements of
meaning, leading nowhere, like stars
sparkling above earth. Whose
clever stars are these, peeking
through fog, or trailing across
empty space, like slow moving
fireworks?
What intern is this, laughing at
the nurses, mocking the surgeons?
What beginnings that don't begin,
really, like starting to have sex
while watching the television.
Sooo, what are we going to watch now?
So can you come over after work?
Like so. Like sooo cool. So? So
I think the hearts of mothers in
Nigeria must be exploding like
bombs when they see their babies
going off to war. So the way
they go on with such dexterity.

Hoodoo

Knowing how silly it is,
still I chase the wind blown hair.

I run it down for blocks,
weaving through briefs and suits.

My heart fills like a rain bucket
with stories from the old people.

Someone took a lock of grandma's hair
and fixed her so she couldn't walk.

Someone made frogs grow in Emma's belly.
Hattie's hair fell out.

I chase it like I'd chase a black cat,
desperate for the bones.

This is who we are. This is everything.
Never being held by strange fingers.

Grind

black boys
on skateboards

hunched over
like wheat.

the grating
roll

and pit bull
stroll.

pants not
pants at all

bright boxers
bounce like

spray painted
cars

bombed and
turning

tracks
from harlem

to brooklyn.
whisper juju

and they roll.
whisper hip

and they hobo
a rail

grinding sparks.
whisper

break
and they weave

each other
in and out.

whisper jitter,
michael

and they dip
and pump

like woodcutters
splitting blocks.

It Could Have Been a BBQ

It could have been a BBQ,
a kind of back yard reunion,
except, there was no food.

> There were men in caps and t-shirts
> and women in heels,
> in skirts so short they
> choked them. They stood
> in streetlit incandescence,
> barely moving.

It could have been a cult,
with all the pistols and Uzis,
except no one surrendered.

> They stood like brick, arms
> crossed, guarding mistakes.
> In the distance, the Oakland
> hills were quiet. I could see
> the headlights of a car, winding
> around, then disappearing.

It could have been my student
banging on the car window
except, she brought me here.

> She used to always sit three seats
> back near the window,
> and daydream. While I
> talked and painted on the
> blackboard, she watched
> leaves waving in the wind.

The Wild Things

Ronnie doesn't know what blackness is.
It mystifies him.
Just reach out and touch it, his friends say.
Hold it, and take it home.
But each time, it evaporates.
He searches the post apocalyptic
cities of hip hop
like rummaging through the
still smoldering ashes
of a house
that just burned down.
He looks for clues in blackface.
Among the suits and ties
in his dying, white
grandfather's closet.
It has to be more than
this slapping of hands. This withheld
breath and slouching
of hips.
He forages the mirror
for fragments of his mother.
Her white glow.
Perhaps it will illuminate
his daddy's black shadow.
When his mother and his father appear
around him in his room at night,
he screams, adrift
on the island of the wild things.

Fishing

You're the one animal
Noah never had to worry about.

There was no flood for you,
no forty days. It was like
for the blind when the lights
go out.

It must have seemed odd, though,
bodies sinking slowly
all around, like confetti,
some still reaching up.

The windows and doors
you could now swim through.
Their spoons left sitting on tables.
Their axes
suffering their own weights.

No man or god ever rescued you,
or bothered to ask
what it is like to swim through
cold light, breathing,
to be here, to have been
here for eternity.

Nineveh

I have not wanted to go to my Nineveh
any more than anyone else.
To touch the space between night and morning,
or better, refract it, as the sky does
like now, with pink striations.

I know I am inside the flesh of something
else, of history, that is inside
something else again, because it
wouldn't board the ship, wouldn't budge.
I know well this inside out.

Like the black man in Texas
tied and dragged behind the truck.
I know the silent guilt inside of bowels.
I know nothing else as hard
as starting out for Nineveh.

I would have to peel my skin off first
and be a traitor to be a saint.
I would have to be a scarecrow that
fell apart. If I lived and I was finally
dropped wet and putrid on the beach,

would I just know what direction to walk in?
Would I just know what to say?
Or would there be another voice inside,
another pair of specs in a cluttered house
I couldn't seem to find?

The Morning Blues

The morning lifts me up
like a lion.
The lid is off!

So much to do,
and every day these gulls.
Every day these clouds.

Every day this grass
tempting me to forget.

If only Patrick Henry
had understood
his words.

Whisps of smoke from
factories. And Emily.
And you too, Rimbaud.

I take an Indian paintbrush
and paint myself green
as a child's voice.

I drink a cup of coffee
and stand in line
to catch the morning train.

But a bakery of something
plum, and jasmine
and seaweed

patchouli and conk
are fire and smoke.
And the slant the street

makes going up between
the thighs of houses
into the hills.

And the echoes through
the tunnels, the foghorns
and don't walk signs.

And a eucalyptus wind
is dropping a whole city
down my throat.

Committed

Someone has stolen
the chicken wire
that keeps the voices caged.

I can't hear a thing.
I am a sail billowed by
wind, but missing the boat.

I am an eighth note,
searching for a scale.
Now wrist bound,

the wind rides up
the white gown
they've put me in.

I try my best to shout,
but the devil's
cold breath settles

like a fog
blanketing buoys
and all of the piers

and the rivers are
so wide on my wrists
I can't make it across.

Why do they keep on
stopping me, anyway,
when I am almost back

to the blue pearl of light,
to Mama, humming
or hanging out clothes?

Asylum

The rules of the asylum
and the lounge are not so different.
Don't let them see your anger.
One will hold you longer then,
the other will escort you out.
Don't let them see your pain.

Forget the beat. No one's going
to dance anyway. Dream,
while there, or not, of being there,
Kalua and cream spilling over
the rocks, hugging them with
a feminine touch.

The devil in the red dress
is gone with the jazz, and if you
talk like your grandma, you'd
better put it in quotes. Run
to catch up. Run to keep up.
Take the drugs.

Push the envelope, but don't
tear it. Brothers are out.
It's no longer 1960, after all.
We can't all win a prize.
We can't all ride the bus.
How many of us will the bus
hold?

Tenure

They chased me down the street with guns,
and so
I came in here,
to hide in robes and chants
like a pickpocket in a monastery.

I'll wear a different mask this time
so as not to starve.

The body'll be polite.
Forego the jive, the motherwit.
Cover up the crucifix
and burn the lotus off my skin.

Pick through heaps
of celluloid
like homeless through trash
for new demeanors.

For as any slave
would tell you, when his toe
is being hacked off for trying to run away,
these are no small things.

Contrary to what people say,
the cock, like the soul,
like the hapless bee
drone does care what blossom it enters.

The Colleague

I smile at you like
a railroad porter
smiling at nice, white ladies
he saw to their seats. Your smile
is a book I cannot open.

The train wheels click
like a clock over the iron rails.
You tell me about the summer house
your great, great grandfather built.
Still standing, still cozy.

Your dog had to have surgery
for a tumor in his throat.
Colorado is so beautiful
this time of year.
The air is like Eden.

My great, great grandfather
also built houses.
But he was a slave.

Then I must be a Negro on a boat
floating down the Mississippi.
When I'm not rowing,
I serve. When I'm not serving
I'm doing a dance.

Sometimes people pitch nickels
in the hat like pennies
in a wishing well.
They note the sounds,
the motions,
the authenticity of the hat.

In their gazes, in their thoughts,
I hang like a portrait.
I am always faint as the wind.

Bayou

a scream
from the bayou.
pumpkin time
and the baby's dabbing
fingers in the mush.
i wish i could hold
a whore, or god, or my sister
when i'm dying like this
smiling, swallowing scraps of iron.
not just cajun, but black.
poor as job's turkey hen,
mama says.
the world is so big,
but so small.
in the swamp are
gators, but in a boat
i bet i could cross it.
baby. let's be born, again.
let's rise out of louisiana.

Geechee

Daddy used to call me geechee.
Lil geechee man.
The rice was the reason.

He thought he'd gotten away
from all of that down home
stuff.

No pig's feet,
chitlins, collard greens, or
corn bread for daddy.

But I felt cassava whispers around
the rice bowl I dove into
and had to have every night.

I felt mojos and cowbells,
palms and guinea dust
in my gravy.

I ate, he said, like I was trying
to get back to my country.

Some of us come from
the right country, daddy said.
Some of us come from
the wrong one.

Building, like daddy

He built our house and it
leaned. Roofed our room
and it leaked
into seven buckets.

We learned to step between
them in the dark,
or brush against them
gently for the sounds
they made
on our way to the outhouse.

Mama put her hands
on her hips, and shook
her head.
But I understood.

On days like this when
the salt blows in from
whale fins, past junipers.

Trying to build cabinets,
but lost inside of pith,
lost inside rings that burn
the fire from my breath
like kindling.

Lessons

Each word you taught to me
you taught to my son.
Not the word, not the
Webster's meaning, but
the will behind it, the will
to cross hidden barriers
like a boy and a horse
across wooden fences.
It's like this with fathers.
No one I know had one who spoke
from the inside out. They make
the masks. They go in the forest
and come out with blood. No one knows
where a father has been, only
that he wouldn't tell if his
life depended on it.

Jewel Dust
For the homeless, Ashanti poet of Venice, Los Angeles, 1990

The life that is in me
like jewel dust,
like porcelain rust
or pepper pot.

Let it sit empty
as a beaten-up cup,
as a broken bowl
in a fallen house.

If it can be still
while the body is skipped
across centuries
like a flat stone

On a lake,
and goes into the world
of white flames
breathing propane,

remembering always
to hold its breath.
If it can go fully clothed
but never be seen.

If it can park here
between the shadows
and the things
and eat and drink

But not fall in
to madness, or dissolve
like the frayed
parchment it is.

The blood can go back
to water, the bones
to threshing floors of
of cane and wheat.

II

Your blood
has always been a blues
looking for itself,

for a flight that will
keep you airborne
as autumn geese.

But you are seized
by patois
and akimbos,

by something atlantic
and are always
pulled back.

In your mind, you see
streets filled with
magnolia,

and pecans among
the palms and palo verde.
You see willows

instead of the litter,
and repatriates
in the crowds and amid

the decadent.
You see our wishes,
I think, but not

our flesh, where
to search, but not
our hunger or our thirst.

            III

The many selves drive the
horses through the rain.
The squalor of frogs
pelting roofs and fronds.
Hard drops battering flesh.
The odor of soaked cloth
like that of cloth in flame.

The many selves start to dance,
with Tai Chi hands and feet,
like waves of lilies in wind
or Santerístas.

Cars zing by on Westwood
and never notice,
any more than white folks did
the old, black, elevator men.

Like Shadrack, Meshek,
and Abednego, they are
somewhere beyond. They are
fire dancing in the torrent,
but never getting wet.

IV

You can't find any roses here.
You can't find any water.
The fruits are dry as stones.

When you bite into them.
When you cut them open,
there is nothing

to be saved by.
Row after polished row
in bright supermarkets,

but not a single ghost,
not a drop of blood, a scent
of rot, not a whisper.

The air is St. Luke.
Houdini. Out of nowhere,
it appears. Grey as a dirty nickel.

If there was a lake, it would
never see its own face.
No one would ever drown in it.

The seaside is St. John
who has never heard of Jesus,
who simply cannot find a reason.
Gun metal glints from a car
window. The speakers rearrange
your bones. Outside, you are

inside something like
a wound, like someone else's
passion, burning alive.

V

Who else can see the spiders
on webs across the abyss,
as tires sing on the 405
three hours before dawn,
and the raccoons and foxes
slink between metal cans
before making their way back
through dried, golden grasses,
but vagabonds, hidden deep here
like blue flame in ether?

Who else can hear the wasps talk
about the withering spores, the
sanctities of the earth
closing like an iris, removed
from light, their cries
shaking the birds awake
and painting
the morning callas?
And who else can stand
beside the bleating trees,
while rocks and fruits
rain on fields of hyacinth
but us, who saw the grass
and the palms dance last night
but then like people, part,
and lined with sweat, turn
like would be actors
who didn't get the parts,
away from the pebbles, away
from the wind?

VI

A tree breaks through the
concrete of the aqueduct,
begging you to enter it.
If a hoodoo man comes
in there, you say, and gets lost
who will find him? Who will
reach in and place a palm
on his belly or buttocks to still
things and center them?

But you looked back
and saw no steps, no trace
of being or of having been.
You looked forward and saw
nothing but gulfs.

And so you stepped into
the trunk. You went down
to the crossroads with no guitar.
You sank and then began
to search for doors,
but couldn't break out.
Standing still, the spirits
belched in your breath.
The moon rose like tides
and you could hear them
from far away, washing over
the landfills and the trestles
and the bedsheets of the
frantic and the driven.
You bathed in lavender.
You snorted leather.
You snapped your fingers
and looked the parts. To be

invisible, you say, is simply
to be seen where
everyone else is hypnotized
by their own shadows.

VII

When we were born, someone
wrote books on our bodies.
At the border of the next century
they collected them, like tickets,
or passports. At the first crossing
we ate secretly torn-out pages
to avoid giving them up.
They were sweeter than cane.
But by the second crossing, things
were seldom saved. A picture
etched on the retina. A sentence
tattooed on a capillary.
The one exception is a scent.
It touches things while we
try naming them and fitting them
into made-up spaces.
It is the symbol C of the verse.
It is in the rose, the birds' nests.
It rises from us like steam.
When we cannot find a rose,
or a bird, it pushes out of our skin
like a bug from a chrysalis, like a
dinghy out of a fog bank, knowing
nothing of longitude or tense.
A shade of garlic, and onion
bulb, crocuses, urine, and mint.
It rises from a woman's hair
and sets the air on fire.
It heals our wounds like talismans.

It waits, like the tree branch
doesn't, really, while we gasp,
flail, and go searching, knowing
the quest is where we always fail.
It is what the forest is made of,
and yet, who can find it?

CPSIA information can be obtained at www.ICGtesting.com
Printed in the USA
LVOW100218300112

266109LV00006B/3/P